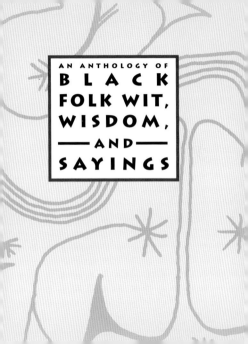

AN ANTHOLOGY OF
BLACK FOLK WIT, WISDOM, — AND — SAYINGS

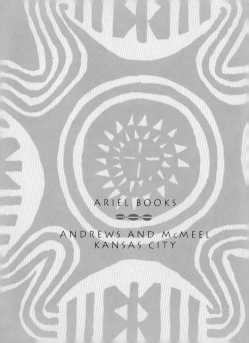

ARIEL BOOKS

ANDREWS AND McMEEL
KANSAS CITY

AN ANTHOLOGY OF

BLACK
FOLK WIT,
WISDOM,
AND
SAYINGS

An Anthology of Black Folk Wit, Wisdom, and Sayings copyright © 1994 by
Armand Eisen. All rights reserved. Printed in Hong Kong. No part of this
book may be used or reproduced in any manner whatsoever without writ-
ten permission except in the case of reprints in the context
of reviews. For information write Andrews and McMeel, a Universal
Press Syndicate Company, 4900 Main Street, Kansas City, Missouri 64112.

ISBN: 0–8362–3064–7
Library of Congress Catalog Card Number: 93–73365

TO MY GRANDMOTHER
ANNIE.

—VC

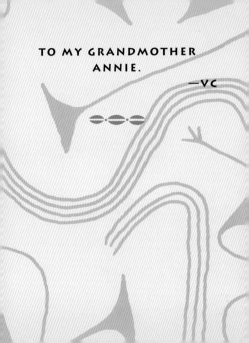

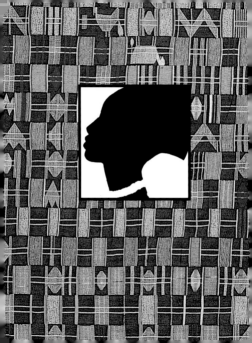

CONTENTS

INTRODUCTION

Wisdom, warnings, advice—all are to be found in the pithy, sharp observations passed down from generation to generation by the elders of a community to guide and instruct its members. Referring to the social mores and habits, even to the animals and foods found in an area, proverbs provide a colorful and poetic picture of a culture and its characteristics.

Though few New World black proverbs can be directly traced to their African origins, some of the cultural roots are obvious. For instance, in Jamaica there are no monkeys or tigers, but both these animals figure in many Jamaican sayings. These proverbs are obviously of African origin.

As an African-American writer, my interest in collecting these proverbs has been not a scientific but a personal one. I have noticed that often, when speaking of morals and manners, the proverbs of a culture seldom display its good points. Instead, they illuminate the pitfalls and stumbling blocks along the road of life—pointing out where others have tripped and helping us to avoid the same mistakes. This is their greatest value and the reason they still have meaning and pertinence to our lives today.

—VANESSA CROSS .

11

ADVERSITY

A stumble is not a fall.

—HAITI

Don't look where you fell, but where you slipped.

—LIBERIA

The stream won't be advised, therefore its course is crooked.

—CAMEROON

The top of the hill is harder to find than the bottom.

—UNITED STATES

AMBITION

The want of a thing is sometimes more than its worth.

—JAMAICA

One who cannot pick up an ant and wants to pick up an elephant will some day see his folly.

—LIBERIA (JABO)

If you want your eggs hatched, sit on them yourself.

—HAITI

A chattering bird builds no nest.

—CAMEROON

Work and you will be strong; sit and you
will stink.

—MOROCCO

COMMON SENSE

Eggs have no business dancing with stones.

—HAITI

As useless as a blind man turning around to look.

—NIGERIA

19

Cows have no business in horseplay.

—JAMAICA

No one tests the depth of a river with
both feet.

—WEST AFRICA (ASHANTI)

It takes a heap of licks to strike a nail in
the dark.

—UNITED STATES

You cannot shave a man's head in his
absence.

—WEST AFRICA (YORUBA)

CONTENTMENT

A dog has four feet but he does not travel four roads at once.

—HAITI

Do not blame God for having created the tiger, but thank him for not having given it wings.

—ETHIOPIA (AMHARA)

23

Being happy is better than being king.

—WEST AFRICA (HAUSA)

Blessed are those who can please
themselves.

—SOUTH AFRICA (ZULU)

FOOLS AND FOLLY

When the mouth stumbles, it is worse
than the foot.

—WEST AFRICA (OJI)

Stupidity doesn't kill you but it makes you
sweat.

—HAITI

The fool looks for dung where the cows
never browsed.

—ETHIOPIA

Whoever heard of a mouse making a nest
in a cat's ear.

—UNITED STATES

FRIENDS AND FOES

An intelligent enemy is better than a
stupid friend.

—SENEGAL

When the hand is full, one has plenty of
company.

—BAHAMAS

27

Make conversation with one who surpasses you, not with one who quarrels with you.

—ZAIRE

Even the tongue and teeth quarrel now and then.

—NIGERIA (NUPE)

28

Hold a friend with both of your hands.
—NIGER/NIGERIA/CHAD

A new broom sweeps clean, but an old broom knows the corners.
—VIRGIN ISLANDS

He who chatters with you will chatter of you.

—EGYPT

Confiding a secret to an unworthy person is like carrying grain in a bag with a hole.

—ETHIOPIA

You can lock your door from a thief, but not from a damn liar.

—VIRGIN ISLANDS

Before healing others, heal yourself.

—THE GAMBIA

You can't carry two faces under one hat.

—JAMAICA

An envious heart makes a treacherous ear.

—UNITED STATES

Rivalry is better than envy.

—ZAIRE

GOOD AND EVIL

Evil enters like a needle and spreads like
an oak tree.

—ETHIOPIA

Evil knows where evil sleeps.

—WEST AFRICA (HAUSA)

GRATITUDE

Thanks cost nothing.

—UNITED STATES (CREOLE)

The one being carried does not realize
how far away the town is.

—NIGERIA

If something that was going to chop off
your head only knocked off your cap, you
should be grateful.

—WEST AFRICA (YORUBA)

JUSTICE

The person who has been a slave from birth does not value rebellion.

—WEST AFRICA (YORUBA)

The tyrant is only the slave turned inside out.

—EGYPT

In a court of fowls, the cockroach never wins his case.

—RUANDA/BURUNDI

He who installs a king never rules with him.

—SOUTHERN AFRICA

The soldier's blood, the general's name.

—JAMAICA

War ends nothing.

—ZAIRE

LIFE LESSONS

Plenty sits still; hunger is a wanderer.
—SOUTH AFRICA (ZULU)

Life is short and full of blisters.
—UNITED STATES

Time is longer than rope.

—VIRGIN ISLANDS

Do more, talk less.

—JAMAICA

Hurrying and worrying are not the same
as strength.

—WEST AFRICA (HAUSA)

LOVE, HOME, AND FAMILY

The ruin of a nation begins in the homes of its people.

—WEST AFRICA (ASHANTI)

Come see me and come live with me are two different things.

—VIRGIN ISLANDS

Tell me whom you love, and I'll tell you who you are.

—UNITED STATES

For news of the heart, ask the face.

—GUINEA

48

If you wish to be blamed, marry; if you
wish to be praised, die.

—ETHIOPIA (GALLA)

One who marries for love alone will have
bad days but good nights.

—EGYPT

What children say, they have heard at
home.

—WEST AFRICA (WOLOF)

A cow gave birth to fire. She wanted to
lick it, but it burned; she wanted to leave
it, but she couldn't because it was her
own child.

—ETHIOPIA

MONEY

Making money selling manure is better
than losing money selling musk.
                                    —EGYPT

A good thing sells itself; a bad thing
advertises itself for sale.
                                    —EAST AFRICA

The spider and the fly can't make a
bargain.

—JAMAICA

Money is sharper than a sword.

—WEST AFRICA (ASHANTI)

Save money and money will save you.

—JAMAICA

When you are rich, you are hated; when you are poor, you are despised.

—WEST AFRICA (ASHANTI)

PATIENCE AND PERSEVERANCE

At the gate of patience, there is no crowding.

—MOROCCO

Restless feet may walk into a snake pit.

—WEST AFRICA

If you wait for tomorrow, tomorrow comes. If you don't wait for tomorrow, tomorrow comes.

—LIBERIA (MALINKE)

The Moon moves slowly, but it crosses the town.

—WEST AFRICA (ASHANTI)

56

Endurance pierces marble.

—NORTH AFRICA

By going and coming a bird weaves its nest.

—WEST AFRICA (ASHANTI)

PRIDE AND VANITY

The noise of the wheel doesn't measure
the load of the wagon.

—UNITED STATES

An empty sack can't stand up; a full sack
cannot bend.

—VIRGIN ISLANDS

A big head is a big load.

—NIGERIA

The price of your hat isn't the measure of your brain.

—UNITED STATES

The drum makes a great fuss because it's empty.

—TRINIDAD

The words of the night are coated with butter; as soon as the sun shines they melt away.

—EGYPT

A beautiful thing is never perfect.

—EGYPT

The face of water is beautiful, but it is not good to sleep on.

—WEST AFRICA (ASHANTI)

You don't have to turn around and look at
every dog that barks at you.

—HAITI

Pride and dignity would belong to women
if only men would leave them alone.

—EGYPT

If there were no elephants in the jungle,
the buffalo would be a great animal.

—GHANA

Put a rope around your neck and many
will be happy to drag you along.

—EGYPT

64

PROVERBS

Proverbs are the daughters of experience.
—SIERRA LEONE

Proverbs are the affairs of the nation.
—ZAIRE

When the occasion arises, the proverb
arrives.

—WEST AFRICA (OJI)

RESPECT

You do not teach the path of the forest to an old gorilla.

—ZAIRE

When you go to a donkey's house, don't talk about ears.

—JAMAICA

Cussing the weather is mighty poor farming.

—UNITED STATES

Cross the river before you talk about the crocodile's mother.

—WEST INDIES

One camel does not make fun of the other camel's hump.

—GUINEA

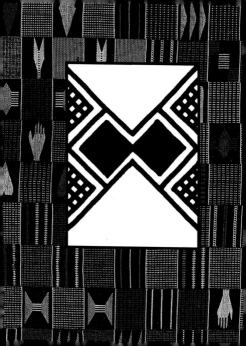

TEMPTATION

Never pick up what you did not put down.
— VIRGIN ISLANDS

The devil tempts but doesn't force.
— GUYANA

WISDOM AND TRUTH

Instruction in youth is like engraving in stone.

—Morocco

Not to know is bad, not to want to know is worse.

—The Gambia

Those who have experienced nothing
mistake the sound of weeping for singing.

—DAHOMEY (EWE)

Seeing is different from being told.

—KENYA

74

The man who goes ahead stumbles so that the man who follows may have his wits about him.

—KENYA (BONDEI)

No one is without knowledge except him who asks no questions.

—CENTRAL AFRICA (FULFULDE)

The shoe knows if the stocking has a hole.

—BAHAMAS

Knowledge is like a garden: if it is not cultivated, it cannot be harvested.

—GUINEA

The truth is like gold: keep it locked up and you will find it exactly as you first put it away.

—SENEGAL

Truth tellers make no mistake.

—EAST AFRICA

Wisdom enclosed in the heart is like a light in a jug.

—KENYA

The gums understand best the teeth's affairs.

—DOHOMEY (EWE)/UNITED STATES

Those killed for lack of wisdom are numerous; those killed by wisdom do not amount to anything.

—NIGERIA/BENIN/TOGA

The text of this book was set in Matrix
and the display was set in Lithos by
Snap-Haus Graphics, Dumont, New Jersey.

Book design by Diane Stevenson /
Snap-Haus Graphics